WHAT IS A LASER?

WHAT IS A LASER?

by Bruce Lewis

Pictures by Tom Huffman

DODD, MEAD & COMPANY, NEW YORK

The term "laserphoto" on page 8 is a trademark
of The Associated Press, Inc.

1 2 3 4 5 6 7 8 9 10

Library of Congress Cataloging in Publication Data

Lewis, Bruce, 1933-
  What is a laser?

  Includes index.
  SUMMARY: Explains what lasers are, how they work,
and some of the amazing things they can do.
  1. Lasers—Juvenile literature. [1. Lasers]
I. Huffman, Tom. II. Title.
TA1682. L48   535.5'8   78-11100
ISBN 0-396-07646-7

To all the helpful people at the
Rochester, Minnesota, Public Library

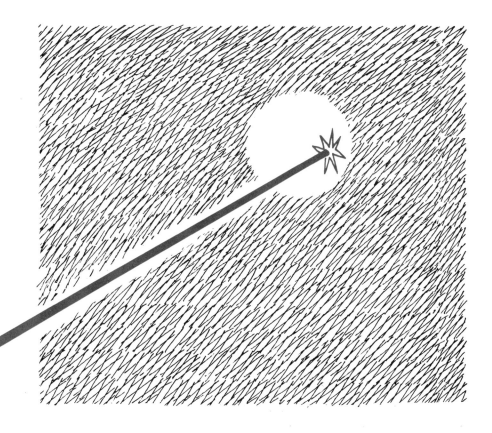

Lasers are the world's most brilliant source of light. Some laser light is brighter than the sun. Powered by supercharged atoms, laser beams can cut and drill materials as hard as diamonds—or be used in delicate eye surgery.

Laser beams can measure the distance from the earth to the moon—or the thickness of a human hair. They are used in making things as different as burglar alarms and baby-bottle nipples. They can carry radio and television signals.

When you see "laserphoto" on a newspaper photograph, you know that a laser helped make the picture clear and sharp before it was sent to the newspaper.

What is a laser?

Like a light bulb, a laser is a source of light. But even if all the light bulbs in the world were turned on at once, the result would not be the same as a beam from a single laser. Laser light is a different *kind* of light. To understand why, let's begin by defining the word "laser" itself.

"Laser" is an *acronym.* This means that it is made up of the first letters of other words. They are:

L ight

A mplification by

S timulated

E mission of

R adiation

Most of these are big words, but their meanings are easy to understand.

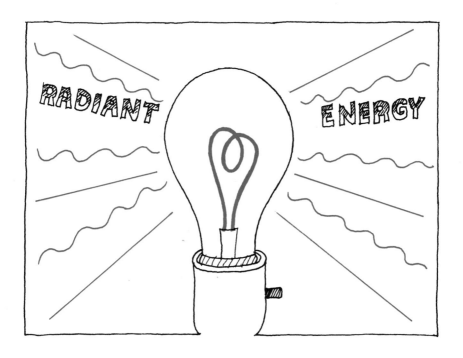

Light is a form of *energy.* You can think of energy as "the ability to get things done." Most energy on earth comes from the sun. When we eat, we get energy from the sunlight our food has absorbed.

It takes energy to make energy. When power plants burn "fossil fuels"—coal and oil—to make electrical energy, they use energy stored by the sun in plants and animals that died ages ago.

We use some of this electrical energy to make light. Light is called *radiant* energy because it flows, or radiates, out from its source.

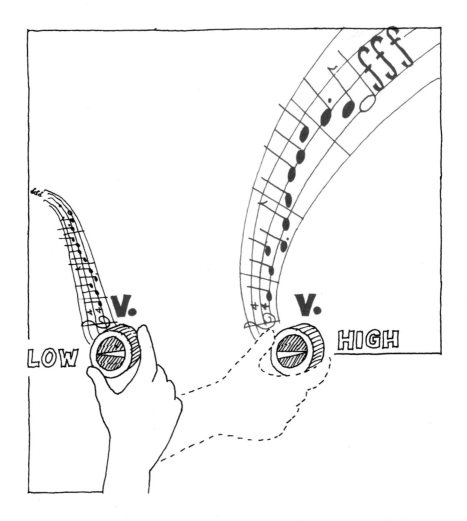

Amplification means to expand something—to make it bigger or stronger. When you turn up the volume control on a television set or radio, you are amplifying the sound. In a laser, amplification means making the light brighter.

Stimulated and *Emission* are two words that go together. They describe an idea that laser scientists borrowed from nature. If the sun can store energy in coal, why not store energy in a laser until there is enough to make a laser beam?

The idea works. A laser is "pumped" so full of light energy that it cannot hold it all. Light particles escape, and as they do, they set free others. In laser language, one light particle *stimulates* the *emission* of another.

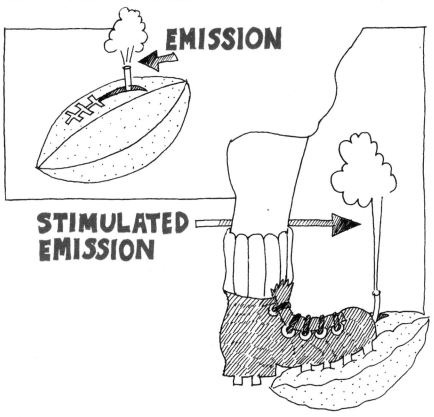

Radiation means that the energy released by the laser is in the form of radiating *light waves.* Sometimes light waves are called *photons,* a word which means a tiny bundle of light. Either way, these particles of light energy radiate outward from their source in a straight line.

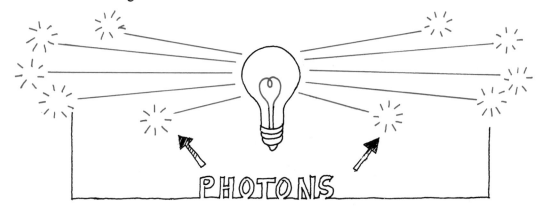

PHOTONS

The word "wave" is used because light actually travels straight ahead by moving up and down. Like a ball bouncing along a long, straight hallway, its forward motion follows a wavy, up-and-down pattern. The distance between "bounces" is called the *wavelength,* and it is different for each color of light.

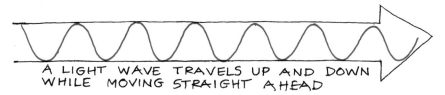

A LIGHT WAVE TRAVELS UP AND DOWN WHILE MOVING STRAIGHT AHEAD

Now let's see how all these ideas go together to make a laser.

12

HOW A LASER WORKS

A laser stores up light energy "under pressure," then releases it in a huge, high-powered burst of light.

You can get an idea of "energy under pressure" by imagining that you are holding a garden hose with its nozzle shut off so that no water can escape. You turn the water on at the faucet and wait for the pressure to build up. Then you open the nozzle all at once, and for just a moment, the stored-up energy in the hose sends the water flying almost twice as far as it usually goes.

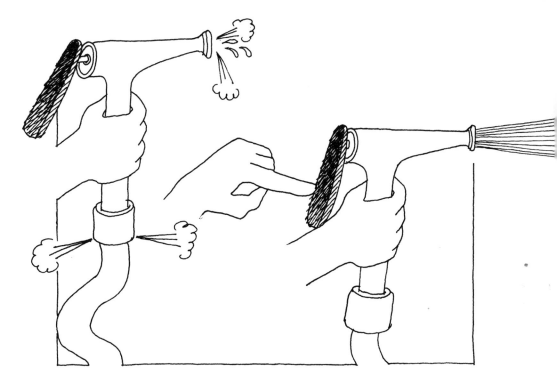

A laser cannot store up light the way a garden hose stores up water pressure. It uses a very different kind of storage system. In a laser, light energy is stored in *atoms*—those tiny particles which make up every kind of material. Atoms are called "the smallest units of matter" because, although they have even smaller parts themselves, none of these parts can be taken away without changing the atom into something else.

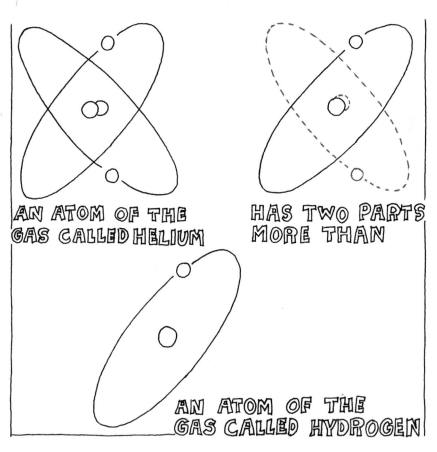

AN ATOM OF THE
GAS CALLED HELIUM

HAS TWO PARTS
MORE THAN

AN ATOM OF THE
GAS CALLED HYDROGEN

Atoms are much too small to see and almost too small to imagine. It takes more than a billion atoms to make a drop of water! But small as they are, atoms are a tremendous source of natural energy, and they play a key role in the operation of a laser.

To understand how a laser uses atoms to store light energy, you can do an imaginary experiment.

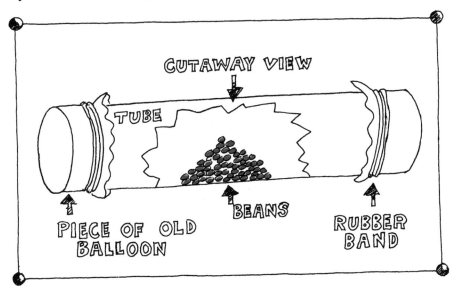

CUTAWAY VIEW

TUBE

BEANS

PIECE OF OLD BALLOON

RUBBER BAND

Suppose you have a cardboard tube about six inches (15 centimeters) long. Inside the tube, put a handful of dried beans—the small, round kind. Cover the ends of the tube with pieces of thin rubber from an old balloon, held in place by rubber bands.

If you shake the tube slowly from end to end, the beans will slide from one end to the other.

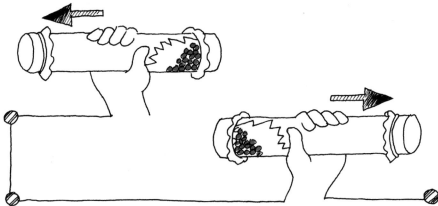

And as you shake the tube harder and faster, you "pump" more energy into the beans. They begin to fly through the air inside the tube. As they bounce off the pieces of rubber at the ends, their energy level grows even more.

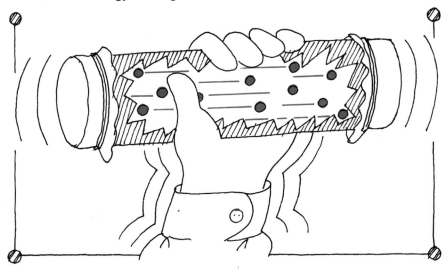

Could you "pump" enough energy into the beans to make them break through the rubber covers? Probably not—unless you made a couple of changes.

A single bean weighs very little. But if you glued all the beans together, all their weight would hit the rubber at the same time. And if you made one of the rubber covers weaker than the other, the combined weight of the bouncing beans would soon burst through it—in much the same way that a laser beam bursts forth from a laser.

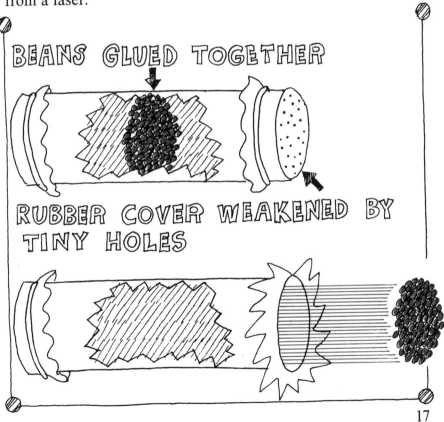

BEANS GLUED TOGETHER

RUBBER COVER WEAKENED BY TINY HOLES

A laser works in a different and more complicated way than a tube full of beans. Even so, there are very few parts in a laser, and they are almost as easy to understand as the parts in your "experiment."

In some lasers, the part that corresponds to the cardboard tube is called the *laser rod.* Laser rods are solid and are made of glasslike materials called *crystals.*

Instead of solid rods, some other types of lasers use hollow glass tubes which contain mixtures of liquids or gases. Using gas-filled tubes to make light is not a new idea. Everywhere we go we see fluorescent tubes with their long cool glow, and neon signs advertising everything from gasoline to groceries. But it takes more than just a tube to make a laser.

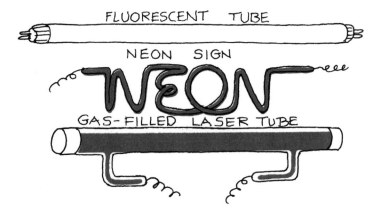

Lasers made with solid rods are "turned on" by a flash of very bright light from a *flash lamp*. The flash lamp works in much the same way as a camera flashbulb, but it can be used over and over.

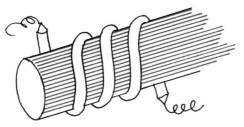

ONE KIND OF FLASH LAMP IS A GAS-FILLED GLASS TUBE WRAPPED AROUND THE LASER ROD.

What happens next is the secret of the laser. The atoms that make up the laser rod itself are put to work, storing up the light energy that creates the laser beam. Long ago, scientists learned that atoms could be excited, or "pumped up," by giving them extra energy from a flash of light.

19

When an atom is "pumped up" in this way, it has more light energy than it should have. This forces it to do something that will return it to its normal condition. It throws off the extra energy as a tiny bundle of light—a photon.

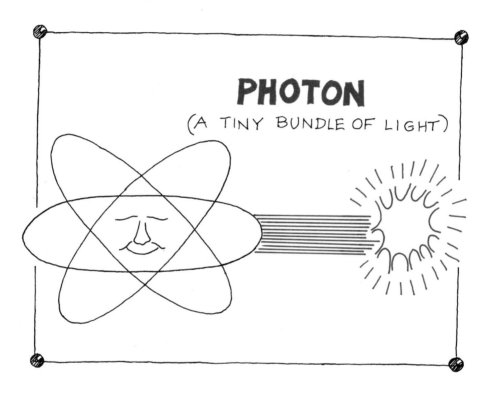

PHOTON

(A TINY BUNDLE OF LIGHT)

The flash of light alone does not create enough photons to make a laser beam. In fact, it does not even excite all the atoms in the laser rod. What the flash lamp does is to make the excited atoms outnumber the ones that are not excited. Then there is a *chain reaction*—something that goes on by itself once it is started.

Here is what happens.

Some excited atoms throw off their photons sooner than others. When a photon bumps into another excited atom, it makes the new atom release its own photon sooner than it would have by itself. This is the part of the laser that is called *stimulated emission*—a giving-out process that is started by something else.

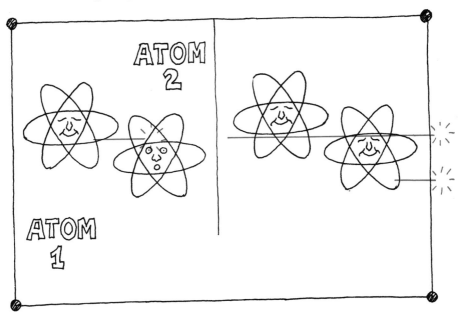

If we could follow just one photon, we would see it bump into another excited atom and knock loose a new photon. Then both photons would bump two more excited atoms, and there would be four photons instead of two. The number of photons would go on doubling at the speed of light. In just 20 "bumps" there would be more than a million of them!

This process is multiplied many, many times, because the flash lamp excites billions of atoms at once. And since each photon set free by the flash can start its own chain reaction, unbelievable numbers of photons are soon flying in all directions.

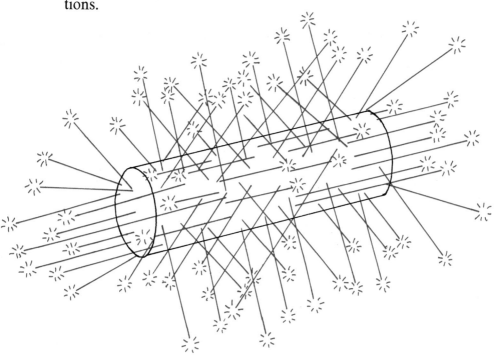

To make a laser beam, most of the photons must be made to move along the center of the laser rod. Then they must be captured before they escape like light from a light bulb. And finally, they must be kept moving so that they can stimulate other photons to move in the same direction.

The first step in solving these problems is to put the laser rod inside a container called a *reflecting box.* Its inner surface is highly polished, like a mirror. It focuses the "pumping" light from the flash lamp into the center of the laser rod so that more atoms will be excited there than anywhere else.

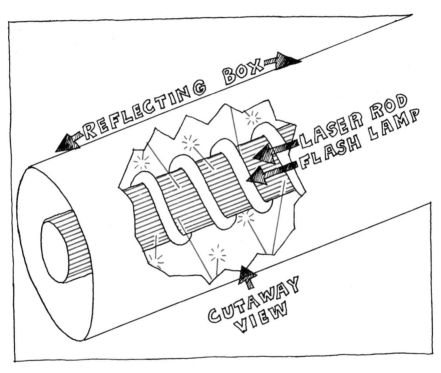

But if photons are allowed to squirt out the open ends of the reflecting box, all the stored-up light energy will soon leak away. To keep this energy "under pressure," there must be a way to keep the photons going back and forth along the center of the rod as the chain reaction builds up.

In our imaginary experiment, we kept the beans in the cardboard tube with pieces of a balloon. But rubber will not bounce light back and forth. What will?

Mirrors, of course. And mirrors are exactly what laser builders use—one at each end of the laser rod. One is a full-strength mirror that reflects everything. The other is weaker, like a mirror you can partly see through because some of the silver backing has worn off.

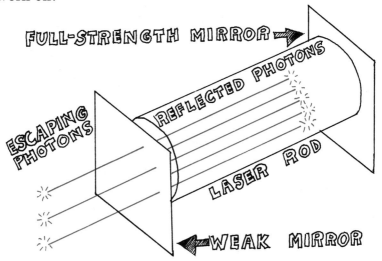

When the photons hit the weaker mirror, some of them escape, but enough others are reflected back into the laser rod to keep the chain reaction going.

Now the photons are trapped inside the reflecting box and between the two mirrors. Their numbers are increasing at a fantastic rate. As more and more of them are generated by the chain reaction in the laser rod, more and more of them escape from the weaker mirror. And when the back-and-forth reflections have lined up the photons so that they are all moving together—like the glued-together beans—the light coming out of the weaker mirror becomes a laser beam.

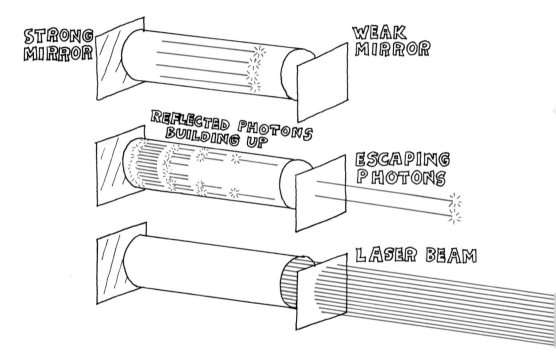

In this type of laser, the beam bursts forth very quickly, but lasts only a fraction of a second. The flash lamp must be set off again to create another beam. Because it operates like the pulsing beat of your heart—pump, rest, then pump again—this type of laser is called a *pulsed* laser.

LASERS AND ORDINARY LIGHT

Now let's look at some of the reasons why laser light is so different from ordinary light.

In a light bulb, atoms in a special wire called a *filament* are excited by electricity. Like the atoms in a laser rod, they begin to release photons.

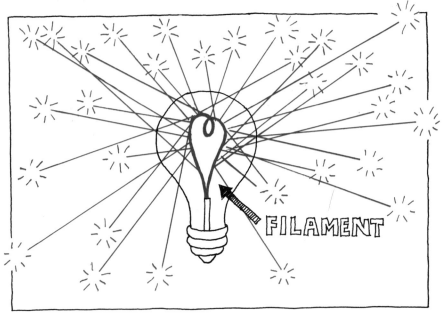

FILAMENT

But unlike the well-organized photons in a laser beam, photons from the light bulb go off at different times and in all directions. There is no way to get them to act upon other atoms in the filament and start a chain reaction—and no way to organize the photons into a concentrated beam.

26

INTENSITY (BRIGHTNESS)

A light bulb's job is just to generate photons and turn them loose. Whenever an atom in the filament is excited, off goes a photon to make light.

But a laser does not let go of its photons right away. It holds them back and builds up "pressurized" light energy. When they are released, they are highly concentrated. There are many more of them than a light bulb could possibly release in the same amount of time.

These extra photons packed into the laser beam give it extra brightness. For this reason, we say that a laser beam has greater *intensity* than any other light source.

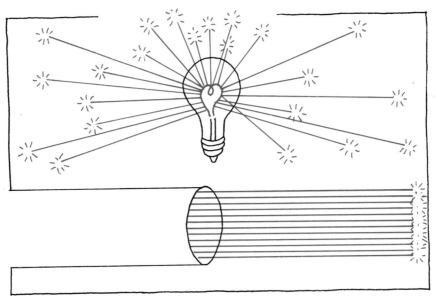

You can think of a laser as a kind of "light gun." It aims photons along the laser rod and "fires" them out of one end like bullets out of a rifle barrel. Because they are all going in exactly the same direction when they leave the laser, the tightly-packed photons in its beam will not "scatter" or spread out the way ordinary light does.

For this reason, a laser beam is said to be highly *directional.* No matter how far it travels, it keeps going in exactly the same direction, and spreads very little.

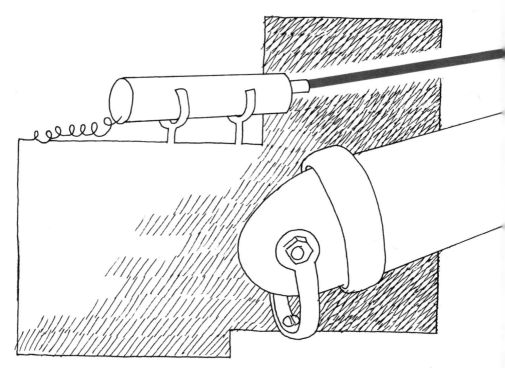

When one of the first laser beams was sent to the moon in 1962, it traveled 250,000 miles and spread to an area only two and a half miles wide. That may seem like a lot, but the very best ordinary light beam we could aim at the moon would spread to an area 100 times wider! Its photons would be so far apart that a person standing on the moon would not be able to see it.

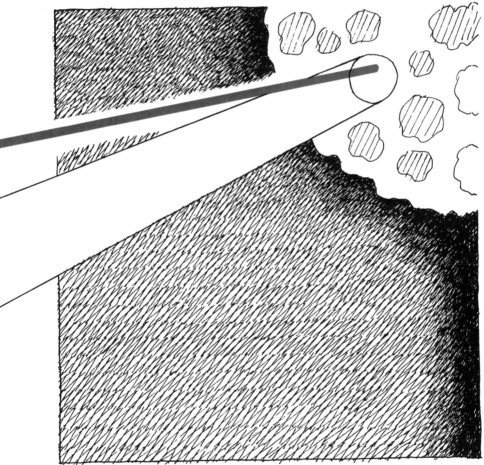

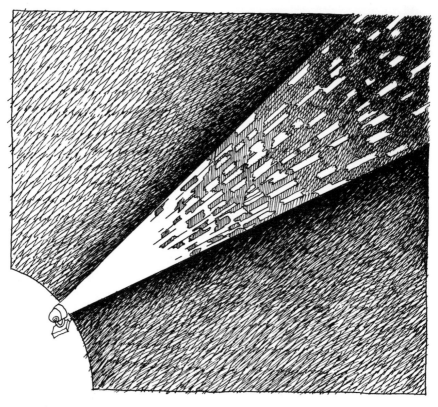

An ordinary light source sends out photons every which way. Some lights—flashlights and searchlights, for example—use reflectors to aim photons in one general direction. But the result is more like a spray than a bullet. And the farther the photons go, the farther apart they get. Soon even the tiniest particles of dust can block their path.

This is why a searchlight seems to stop in mid-sky. Yet the laser beam that went to the moon was strong enough to reflect back to earth. Why?

One reason is that there is a lot more light coming out of the laser to begin with. And it gets off to a better start than ordinary light.

The big difference has to do with the way the light is *organized.* Imagine a football team coming onto the field. The players come out one at a time or in twos and threes, running at different speeds and in different directions. Ordinary light behaves in much the same way as it comes from its source. Its photons are all in a jumble, starting out at different times and headed in different directions, getting farther and farther apart as they go.

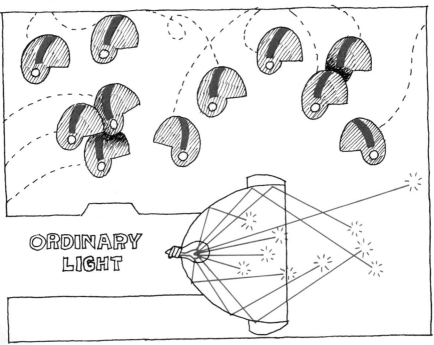

ORDINARY
LIGHT

Laser light is more like a marching band. When the band comes on the field, all the players are marching in the same direction and at the same speed. They are all "in step." And even if they marched for miles, as bands often do in parades, they would stay about the same distance from one another.

The photons in laser light are organized in much the same way—all lined up together, evenly spaced, and exactly in step. For this reason, laser light is called *coherent,* which simply means "well organized."

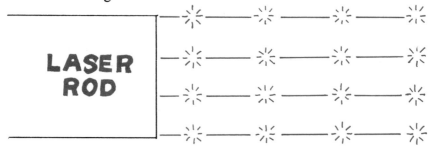

Coherent light is easier to understand if you think of it in terms of light waves. An ordinary light source generates photons at different times and sends them off in different directions. Its light waves move independently—not together.

The result is similar to what happens when you throw a handful of pebbles into a pond. Each pebble makes a wave of its own, but the ripples are small and weak, and soon disappear.

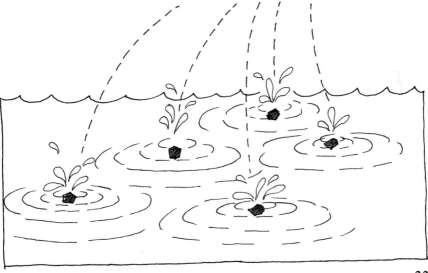

But if you dropped the pebbles into the pond one by one, in the same place each time, you would soon have a lot of circular ripples growing wider and wider as each one was pushed along by the one behind it.

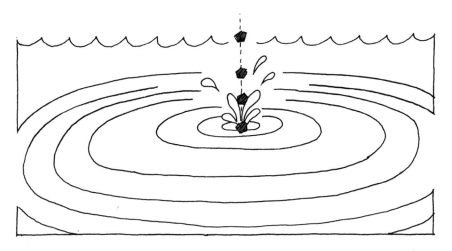

The same sort of thing happens when a light wave bumps an excited atom, "pushing along" a new light wave that immediately falls in step with the first one. Because all the light waves in a laser beam are lined up in this way, laser light can travel farther, stay brighter, and will spread less than light from any other source in the world.

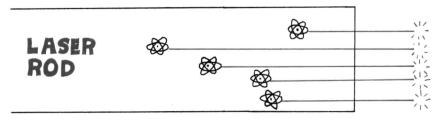

LASER
ROD

RODS, TUBES, AND LASER POWER

The pulsed lasers—those that use solid crystal rods and whose beams flash rapidly on and off—were the first to be developed. The very first one was built in 1960, using a ruby crystal rod about four centimeters long.

Because of its "on-off" operation, this type of laser can have tremendous power. Each burst of light from its laser rod can be as much as 10 million times more powerful than an ordinary light bulb! The heat created by this kind of power would soon burn up the laser if it were left "on" all the time.

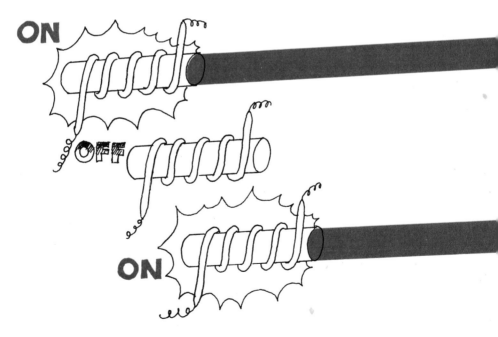

The beam from a gas-filled laser tube generates less power and heat, and can be left "on" all the time. It is usually "pumped" by a constant flow of electricity, which excites the atoms in the gas the way a flash lamp does in a crystal rod. And although gas lasers use very little power—in some cases, less than a flashlight—their continuous beams have more practical uses than the "on-off" variety.

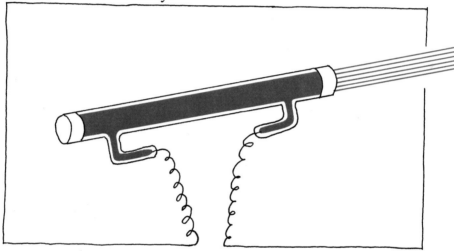

How big is a laser? It depends on the kind of rod or tube that is used. The largest ruby crystal rods are about as big around as a broomstick, and 12 to 18 inches (30 to 45 centimeters) long. Gas lasers can be huge. A gas laser was once built that was more than half as long as a football field!

But a laser does not have to be huge to be powerful. And a laser does not have to be either huge or powerful to be useful.

If you have ever focused the sun's rays through a magnifying glass on a piece of paper, you know what happens when you concentrate a lot of light on one tiny spot. Multiplied many times, the same thing happens when a solid object is struck by the beam from a high-powered laser.

Racing along that beam are billions of photons. When something gets in their way, they pile up in huge numbers. The result is a fantastic amount of energy focused on one small spot. The temperature at that spot instantly rises higher than the temperature of the sun's surface!

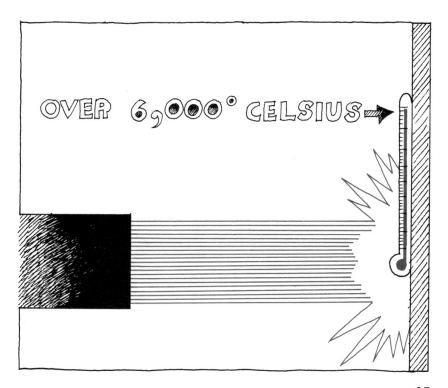

It is no wonder that when lasers were new, they were used mostly for cutting, drilling, and welding jobs. High-powered laser beams can shatter solid rock, punch holes through the hardest steel, or weld large pieces of glass together without cracking them.

Because they use impractical amounts of power and generate impractical amounts of heat, big laser jobs like these are not as common now as they once were. Today, we find more and more laser beams being scaled down in power. They are focused through lenses to cut, drill, and weld on a much smaller scale. The lower power reduces the heat created by the laser beam. The beam can then do its work without burning up the material it is working on.

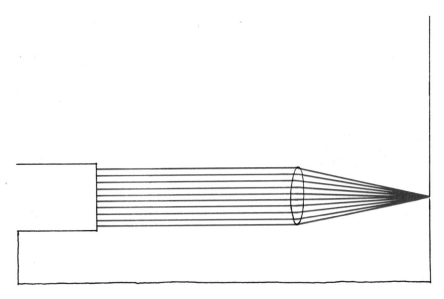

Laser beams controlled in this way are so sensitive that they can drill holes through a human hair. But they have practical uses, too.

They can pass safely through the clear glass of a television picture tube to heat up and weld the wires inside it. They can make hair-sized cuts in delicate materials that would be damaged by other cutting tools. They can weld connections used in computer parts so small that workers need microscopes to watch the welding.

Doctors are using the laser, too. In eye surgery, a carefully controlled laser beam can do things ordinary surgical tools cannot do without injuring the eye.

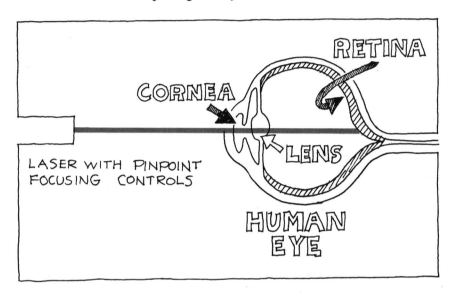

A very delicate part of the eye called the *retina* captures images of the things we see. In some kinds of eye disease, the retina comes loose from the back of the eye, causing poor vision. When this happens, a low-power laser beam the size of a pinpoint can repair the damage. It passes safely through the clear parts of the eye because there is nothing in them to block its path and cause heat. But when the beam hits the retina, the photons pile up, "welding" the damaged area back in place.

Many of the laser's uses have nothing to do with its heat and cutting power. Laser beams with very low power make excellent

40

range finders. (Finding the range of an object means finding out how far away it is.)

Laser range finders work in much the same way as *radar,* a system which can tell how far away an object is by measuring the time it takes a radio signal to get there and back.

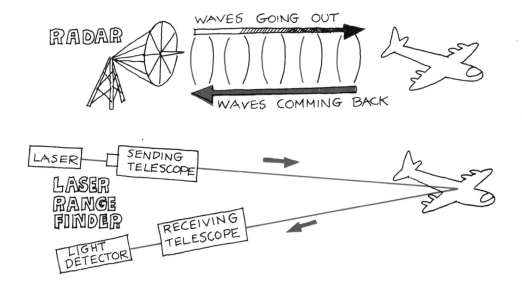

Radio waves are bigger than light waves and get weaker as they travel because they run into more interference. But laser range finders can be used over great distances. They are even used to keep track of rockets and satellites. On the ground, they are used for accurate measurements in land surveys and construction work. And in the laboratory, a laser measuring device has been used to measure the space between two atoms!

Laser beams can also be used like radio waves to send communications signals (telephone, television, and radio). Astronauts in space have communicated to earth over a laser beam. Space is better than the earth's atmosphere for laser communications. In space there are no clouds, rain, snow, or smog to weaken the laser beam's power.

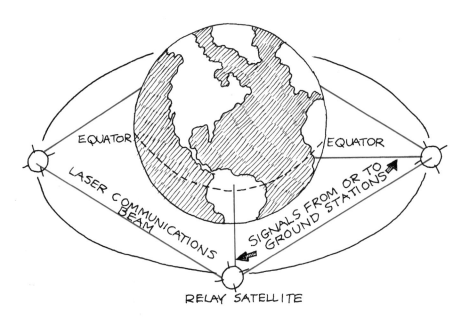

RELAY SATELLITE

The United States Air Force is working on a space communications system with satellites that relay radio and television signals around the world on laser beams. Although the Air Force system is for military use, a system like it may someday be used for better worldwide communications of all kinds.

42

Here are some examples of the many different ways in which lasers can be used.

• A manufacturer of baby-bottle nipples is using a laser system for drilling holes in the ends of the nipples.

• Musical groups—from popular bands to symphony orchestras—are performing "light shows" that use laser beams set to music.

• Art experts are using laser cleaning tools to remove blackness and decay from ancient marble statues.

• Police and security guards can set up low-power lasers well below eye level, so that anyone walking through the beams will set off a burglar alarm.

One thing all these people have in common is the caution with which they handle lasers. Even a low-power beam must be carefully controlled and used with proper safety precautions.

One of the laser's most fascinating uses is a process called *holography*. "Holo" means "whole," and "graph" means "picture." Together, they mean "a picture of the whole thing." And that is what a holograph appears to be—a three-dimensional image.

When an ordinary camera takes a picture of a dog, it records the dog's image on film. The result is a photograph that shows the dog in two dimensions—height and width, but not depth.

In holography, laser light "takes the picture." Behind the dog is a mirror which reflects the laser light toward a piece of film. Instead of an image of the dog, the developed film will contain a record of the light waves that were reflected from the mirror combined with those that were reflected from the dog's body.

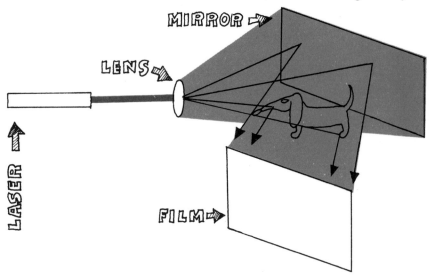

The film is called a *hologram.* You can look through it like a slide or negative, but you cannot see the dog until the film is lit up by a laser. Then you see a three-dimensional image of the dog on the other side of the film. Why? Because you are seeing the same light reflections you would see if you were looking at the dog itself.

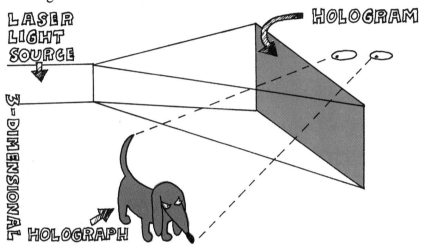

LASER LIGHT SOURCE

HOLOGRAM

3-DIMENSIONAL HOLOGRAPH

Holograms have many uses in business and industry. Some companies are using them for three-dimensional advertising. Engineers make holograms of moving machine parts to look for hidden wear and vibration.

But holograms can also be used for fun. For around $1,000, you can have a holographic portrait taken. And there is even a coin-operated game in which you can "shoot it out" with a holographic movie film of a three-dimensional gunfighter!

These are just some of the ways in which the laser is being used. Right now, no one knows how much more it can do. It is still fairly new, and scientists are still experimenting with it. The laser, they say, "harnesses the power of the universe."

What they mean is that the laser puts nature to work for human beings. It releases and controls the natural power that exists in every atom.

For that reason alone, the laser is a remarkable scientific discovery. It is a valuable and practical tool that is highly useful to us today—and promises to be even more so in the future.

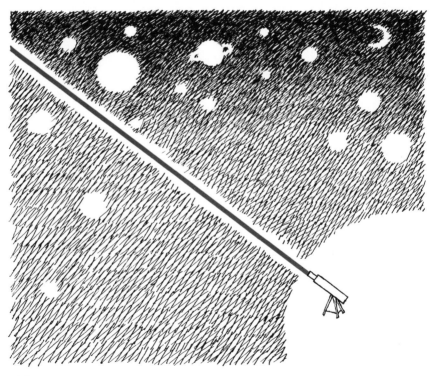

INDEX